WHY SHOULD I WAIT?
When God Said Go!

WHY SHOULD I WAIT?
When God Said Go!

Janice Fountaine

Copyright © 2004 by Janice Fountaine. All rights reserved.

Printed in the United States of America

Publishing services by Selah Publishing Group, LLC, Indiana. The views expressed or implied in this work do not necessarily reflect those of Selah Publishing Group.

ISBN 1-58930-128-5
Library of Congress Control Number: 2004093071

I would like to dedicate this book to my Lord and Savior Jesus Christ. It is because of Him that I live.

I would also like to dedicate this book to all the broken, bound, and hopeless women who are blessed because of the ministries of empowered women who would not wait when God said "go!" I thank Him for impregnating me with a vision for these women and giving me the grace to fulfill it. Knowing this:

A charge to keep I have,
A God to glorify.
  – Charles Wesley

ACKNOWLEDGEMENTS

❖

I would like to thank my husband, Darnell Fountaine, whose love and submission to God has allowed him to see my vision as a part of God's vision for our lives.

I would like to thank my precious mother, Lenora Battle, who has shown me an example of a strong, loving and compassionate woman of God.

I would also like to thank my mother-in-law, Dora Brantley, whose support and encouragement I greatly appreciate.

CONTENTS

❖

Introduction

❖

Many women today are impregnated with vision-vision that has been given to them by God. Yet few of these women can be found in delivery rooms of shelters, transition homes, prisons, and other places where the severely broken frequent.

They have not given birth to their vision because they have not accepted their call to go into ministries and do what God has ordained them to do. Instead, they are filling the vestibules of big churches and conferences year after year, waiting to be released into something that only laboring in God's vineyard could produce.

Some women have even gone to their graves without fulfilling the destiny that God has preordained for their life. The sad part about it is that they knew that they were pregnant, yet never brought forth the vision God had given them. Oh yes, pregnant, ready to breathe, by the power of the Holy Spirit, the breath of life into lost souls. Yet God knows them as having been stagnated, unproductive, and not having fulfilled their purpose in life.

Do you want this to be you? What are you waiting for? Will your vision end up lying in the annals of time aborted or stillborn because you were waiting for someone to give you permission to go? Someone other than God? Someone-a pastor or even a spouse-to validate your call and give you permission to do what God called you to do? Waiting, while the souls of broken women from all walks of life are begging to be set free from the bondage of sin and low self-esteem.

Why? Why should one, even a woman, wait for someone to give her permission to do what her Creator has called her to do? Why wait for someone to play God in your life? Why empower someone else to have control over your future, your soul, your eternal destiny? Why?

A few years ago I repeated these questions over and over again in my mind and spirit as I pondered over whether or not to go into ministry. It was such an issue, a mind-boggling, life-changing decision to make. I felt as though I was going to burst. The call on my life to preach the gospel of Jesus Christ was strong and the vision was clear. It was a call that far exceeded my comprehension, reasoning, and level of growth and maturity in the Lord. A call I knew that if I were sincere about fulfilling God's purpose in my life, I could not wait to answer.

And why should I? If God had not spoken to me. If He had not expressed *His will* and given *His Instructions,* that would have been one thing, but He had and that was what counted. The calling to birth a church was a ministry that ideally my husband should have been starting. Yet, God was calling me, the woman.

Why Should I Wait? is bound to be controversial and even offensive to those who don't understand, and those who refuse to acknowledge the power of God in operation, even when things may appear to be contrary to their understanding of His Word.

Why Should I Wait? is also bound to be disappointing to those women in Christ who search for an excuse to support their innermost desires to preach, teach, or engage in ministry against their husbands' or other's advice.

Instead, this book has been written to encourage and enlighten and support women of God who have truly received a call to pursue a ministry. *Now! Why Should I Wait?* is written to help women understand the urgency for them to step out into uncharted waters, despite the obstacles that lie beneath their feet. And in doing so, they believe that God will work things out. Oh yes! That husband, that pastor, or even yourself, will come to know that your vision is indeed God's vision for you.

I dared to go. I dared to be different. I dared not to wait. I dared because of whom I serve, whose I am, and the words that God spoke to me. "Just go, even if you have to go alone. You do what I have instructed you to do and I'll take care of everything and everyone else."

❖

Like Fire in My Bones

"Then I said, "I will no make mention of Him, nor speak anymore in His name." But His word was in my heart like a burning fire shut up in my bones; I was weary of holding it back, and I could not."

Jeremiah 20:9

People are quick to judge and give you their opinion. What they don't understand, however, is that when God places a calling on your life and tells you to go, there is an indescribable, uncontrollable desire to be obedient and submit to His call. There is a desire to do what He calls you to do. I asked my brother Rev. V. DuWayne Battle, Ph.D. "How do you know when God wants you to do something?" He replied, "When He won't let you *not* do it."

My sisters in Christ, I have found these words to be not only profound but true. The desire to please God was like fire shut up in my bones. When the anointing of God is upon you to do something, you will not be able to sustain yourself. You will have to experience being broken in the areas of your life that are affected by the calling and specific anointing upon your life at that time.

The Holy Spirit nudged at the very intellectual, self-reasoning, disobedient, and faithless part of me that feared and procrastinated. At the time I did not realize that I was on a time schedule and I could not wait. Oh, yes, when God tells us to do or not to do something, it is seasonally timed and intertwined with His overall purpose for His church, even though individually we are as sand on the seashore.

I was reluctant to go because I wanted my husband, Darnell, to go first. But who went first was not my decision. As a matter of fact, I didn't go first. We went out together. I believe that when one goes, to a certain extent, the other goes also. I also believe that God will not have one go without the other being in accord. If your spouse is not in agreement when you receive your call, God will bring him under subjection to Him before you take the step. Otherwise, you must not go and, even more, you must be sure of the call.

I was restless and unsettled. I felt as though I was being pressure-cooked. God would not allow me to be comfortable while I was in a disobedient state. He would not let me say no. His picture is far bigger than our woes and fears. It is not an option when you are sold out to God.

If you feel you must deny the call of God for whatever reason, His Word, will become like fire in your bones and you will eventually have to go. God has placed in you an immense desire not just to do the work He has called you to do, but to please Him. And to please God is to obey Him when He calls-no matter what the cost.

The application of fire is to cause or provoke someone or something to undergo a process of purification. It will burn up the very fiber and materials within us that cause us to fear or oppose doing what God has called us to do. But, even in the midst of opposition or the fiery trial, you will emerge, with spiritual maturity, boldness, and confidence. The opinions of others or your selfish ways of doing things will not move you. Instead, you will come forth proclaiming what indeed is God's will concerning you.

Will God Call Women into Ministry?

"And the angel answered and said to her, The Holy Spirit will come upon you, and the power of the Highest will overshadow you"
LUKE 1:35A

I think, ministry is one of the most controversial subjects in Christian circles. The battle over whether or not God would call a woman to preach, even to pastor, is still being fought among clergy and lay people throughout the churches of God. Marriages are damaged, friendships are broken, and church conferences are split-each side giving numerous arguments to either support or dispute their claim as to whether or not God would call women into ministry.

I believe the most popular argument stems from the Apostle Paul's statement in 1 Timothy 2:12 that women should "be in silence" in the church. Many men have used this passage of Scripture to stroke their egos when, in actuality, they have robbed God of the real effect this verse was to have on the life of Christians.

Paul's proclamation that women should keep silent in the church was to address issues that had nothing to do with God's desire to call women into ministry.

Another argument is that if God intended for women to lead, then Jesus would have chosen a woman disciple. When I myself did not believe in women in ministry, I supported this argument. But when God spoke to me, I obviously needed some answers. God told me that He chose me and I did not have to validate my calling to preach to anyone. In the time of Christ, it was more feasible for men to adjust to the lifestyle of a disciple because of the culture. They would be more easily accepted and the prevalence of women coming into ministry had its season just like everything else under the sun.

The best, most profound, and indisputable argument I can give you, is the fact that God spoke to me and has anointed me. I know His voice and walk in His power.

God chooses the vessel, not man. His manifested power gives credence to any argument. It gives support to the genuineness of Christianity. When people ask how I know Christianity is genuine, I tell them in one word: *power*. Christianity is the only religion that is accompanied by the yoke-breaking power of God.

So it is with many women in Christ. The yoke-breaking power of God is upon their lives and it is His will that they adhere to the great commission in Matthew 28:19 as well as any male: "Go ye, therefore, and teach all nations" (KJV). Although I believe that God may use the community of faith to corroborate ones call, no individual needs another person to validate or make authentic what God has spoken to them. *God is concerned with lost souls. He is not concerned with the gender of who pulls the dying out of a ditch.* If the truth be told, let one of those who argue that God will not call a woman to preach be faced with the decision as to whether they want a woman to pull their dying mother or father, sister or brother, son or daughter out of a ditch, one minute before the Rapture. And in order for her to pull that person all the way out, she has to nurture him with the exhorted Word of God. Do you really think that those who argue will say no, that God will *not* call a woman to proclaim to a lost soul, one minute before the Rapture, that Jesus Christ loves them and is coming back?

A call to preach goes far beyond the pulpit. It stretches way past the bishop's ring and the apostle's rod. It outshines the usher's pin and the choir's robes. A call from God seeps through the depths of the outer gates and pours out onto the harvest where the saturation of His love and grace awaken lost souls. A call to preach, a call to any type of ministry, says "I will not wait, because God says go!"

❖

To Everything There Is a Season

"To every thing there is a season, a time for every
purpose under heaven"
ECCLESIASTES 3:1

It was a cold rainy day in December, in Washington, D.C.
After the Sunday morning worship service at our home
church, my husband Darnell and I stood in front of a building that had previously been a liquor store, and claimed it
for the church God had instructed me to start. We soon
learned, however, that what we claimed was not ordained by
God, so, we kept looking. I knew the church would be in this
vicinity as God had shown the area to me in a vision and I
could not wait.

About two weeks later, around mid-afternoon, I drove on
that same street to look at another space we were considering renting for Sunday services. This building seemed perfect
for a church. As a matter of fact, I learned it was actually
used as a church before, but the new owner was using it as a
multiactivity rental space. This I found to be quite discom-

forting. I couldn't see us using God's money to support an organization I knew would reinvest the funds in ungodly activities such as parties, discos, etc.

While en route home, the Holy Spirit instructed me to go try a new route-one that, although I had been told was quicker, I had never traveled on my own. About one block after turning the corner, the Holy Spirit spoke to me again saying, "Look to the left," and there it was! I saw a lady turning the key in the lock of a storefront church. I immediately parked the car and went and knocked on the door of the church. She answered, we talked and I learned that she was in the process of packing up. She had decided to hold church services from her home. I perceived her to be a holy woman of God, from her outward showing of love and kindness, and I will always thank her for allowing God to use her. She offered me items from her church that she would not need any longer. She supplied me with the owners telephone number, and she encouraged me in the ministry. Her name is Rev. Rita Martin. Rev. Martin has since worshipped with us on occasion and I have had the opportunity to preach at her home church.

Meeting Rev. Martin was an ordained event in each of our lives. It was an appointed time relative to God's purpose for our lives. It was a season.

Life is full of seasons and every divine event in the life of a Christian has been appointed a season. A set time for planting and a set time for fruition. These seasons are periods that will come whether we are ready for them to or not. What we must always remember is that what God has ordained will come to pass. After spring there is summer, after summer there is fall, and after fall there is winter.

You may not buy an umbrella, but the spring showers will come.

You may not have air conditioning, but the summer heat will come.

You may not buy a rake, but the fall leaves will fall.

You may not have you car winterized, but the winter cold will come.

You may not prepare yourself to be used by God, but the season, the ordained time for God's ministries will come and if you are not in place God will use someone else. Perhaps someone whom you least expect.

It's not about us. It's all about God and His will. As a matter of fact, God has not even made himself the focal point, but lost souls. Jesus said *"I have come that they might have life and have it more abundantly."* John 10:10 In other words, Jesus said, I came through forty-two generations, took on the body of man and at the same time kept the essence of the Father. I permitted the devil to place a crown of thorns on my head, refused to discharge the angels while I was being despised, rejected, scourged, and wounded, and caused myself to be lifted and crucified. In essence, God set redemption on a mantle called Calvary so that sinful mankind could be drawn back into fellowship with Him. Now the lost can be found, the captives can be set free, and the foolish can become wise.

The season for Word of God Ministries to be planted had come. It is the ministry that God had ordained while Darnell and I were in our mother's wombs. Yes, our season had come and someone had to move. Lives had to be changed and captives had to be set free. Parents and grandparents were praying. People were waiting to see Jesus. The season had even come for them to experience change in their lives, and God told me to go. So, why should I wait?

❖

Be Sure of Your Call

Therefore, brethren, be even more dilligent to make your call and election sure.
2PETER 1:10

You must be sure of your call. The operational ministry, purpose, and assignments that God has predestined for you, and makes known to you through the Holy Spirit, cannot be based on your desire to pursue a particular ministry. It cannot be based on hunches, feelings and emotions, past experiences, people's opinion, or even a pastoral selection. It must be from God and Him only. You may have a desire to pursue a particular ministry. Your pastor may say that he or she needs you in a position and people may tell you that you look good in that certain position. You, your pastor, and other people may say that it was made for you. But the question to you is, did God call you or did you and others call you?

Your call into any ministry must be based on a divine revelation, personal word directly to you from God. That's one reason why it's so important for us to lay before God in worship and fervent prayer daily. We should be in solitude daily, away from people and other interference so we can commune with Him and Him with us. Our problem is that we are so use to praying at the end of the day when the body is tired and weary from life's daily activities. At which time, we make our petitions to God. That's if we don't fall asleep first. Then we end our prayer without allowing God a chance to respond to it. Don't you think that it's rude to ask someone a question or favor and not give them an opportunity to answer? Then because we haven't heard from God, we depend on others to give us a word from Him and when they tell us something we take it and run. Never mind if we didn't receive a word directly from God.

Be sure of your calling. The Holy Spirit will reveal it to you. What others say should be a confirmation of what God has spoken to you; however, the call should come to you first. Some people will say that they had to tell you because you were not listening to God. But, will God call someone into a ministry who hasn't yet reached the level of maturity to listen to Him? What happens when He wants to give them further instructions?

When someone approaches you with a Word from God, even if it seems as though you're hearing it for the first time, you're not. It should be a confirmation. If it's not, then you should examine the prophecy. You may be running from your calling from God or trying to ignore it. Whatever the reason, deep down you know God has spoken to you about it in your spirit. As a matter of fact, more than likely, your spirit was already beginning to hunger and thirst after answering God's call in doing the ministry.

On the other hand, if your pastor or someone else speaks to you about going into a ministry that you don't have a compassion for or that you don't feel comfortable with, God may not have spoken it. You had better not go, you had better wait. You should lay before the Lord and be sure of your call. Be mindful, though, that if your pastor wants to elevate you to a leadership position, then you are probably at a level spiritually where you should be doing something.

To enter into a ministry based on a personal desire or what has been spoken in your life is a tragedy. We think some ministries are in the limelight, so we desire to be there too. You must examine yourself as to why you are so adamant to enter into a ministry that God has not spoken directly to you about. Lay before God. Emotions may have been blurring your vision, nevertheless, The Holy spirit will let you know. Separate yourself through fasting and prayer until you hear from God, who would not have you confused or misled. He will speak. And He will speak to you directly.

Be sure of your call. It's of utmost importance. It will affect your relationship with God. If you go when you are not sure, doubt will plague you and taunt you, and you'll never be sure of your ministry. There's a strong possibility that you'll fall on your face and bring others down with you. Most of all, you will be out of place and out of God's will. God will not reap his ordained glory from your life and ministry.

I was sure, without a doubt, of my call from God to start a church ministry. He spoke to me directly during my daily morning prayer. In His soft and loving but authoritative voice He told me.

"You are my angel, watch over My people. I'll tell you whom, what, where, when, and how. People are waiting to see Me. They want to see Jesus. Just give them My Word, give them Jesus. Prepare the way for the Lord, for the King of Glory shall come in."

So when others questioned my call, even my husband, all that I could say was I know God called me. I know the voice of God. I have received a direct personal word from God and it would have been inexcusable for me to let anyone deter me from accepting the call and entering into Pastoral ministry.

No, I didn't fully understand why God chose me, why He decided to give me the vision when He did, but as far as I was concerned, I didn't have to understand fully. I was sure of my call. I acknowledge God as my Creator and Lord and understand that I am a created vessel. God is God and my desire and endeavor to obey Him is not predicated on my comprehension of His intentions, motives, and ways of doing things. I know that in God's appointed time, I will understand why He does things the way He does. But as for then as well as now, God doesn't owe me an explanation because of who He is. He is God. God is never indebted to us; He does not owe us anything. I admit it would have been much easier for me if He had shown my husband the big picture in the beginning, but He didn't and that was His choice. He is God.

As Christians we must learn how to trust and obey God, especially when others don't understand. I know it's easier to obey when you understand. But when you understand, your faith is not challenged. Understanding while seeing supports the principle of what we see is what we believe. It is trusting while knowing, an act that does not embrace faith at any level. Instead it clarifies only the physical. But faith clarifies or understands the spiritual. It gives credence to what you are doing, even though the physical eye can't comprehend or reason with it.

My husband viewed what I said was a call from God into the pastoral ministry as an act of taking a leadership role in our home and relationship. And no matter how much I denied this accusation, he would not believe otherwise. Only a revelation from God could convince him. But I knew within myself that when God called me to pastor, pastoring was the farthest thing from my mind. As a matter of fact, I wanted to evangelize. I wasn't even a people person and I had no desire to be in a leadership position, thus I knew even more that it was God who spoke to me. As I quoted earlier, you'll know when God wants you to do something, it is when He won't let you *not* do it. In other words, God can make you feel so uncomfortable while you're not doing it that you will yield to His will.

My foremost desire was, and still is, to do the will of God in my life and to please Him. When God called me, to some people, it meant going out before my husband, but I could not wait because God said "go." Why should I?

People Will Talk

"Out of the same mouth proceed blessing and curs-
ing." My brethren, these things ought not to be so."
JAMES 3:10

Talk is cheap. Stay focused. No matter what situation, person, event or problem is before you, God must always be in front of it. This way He will be all that you see. You cannot be distracted with God in front. Certain distractions will blur your vision, but if you stay focused on God, He will take care of everything for you.

One of the tools the devil uses to distract us is talk. People will talk; there's no doubt about it. It's man's nature. They will automatically think the worse, hear the worse, and say the worse. If you are focused on God and what He has told you to do, you are always aware that there is no time for side issues or for anything that is not of Him.

You cannot get wrapped up in others' opinions or unspiritual reasoning. Man's reasoning cannot begin to comprehend the thoughts and logic of God. They will not understand and they probably will not agree either. So why wait for them to? As a matter of fact, you can't let them influence you one way or the other.

Some talk is meant to help you and some is meant to hurt. Some people will have good sounding advice or just good sounding comments. But no matter how well it sounds and works for others, the only thing that will work for you is what God said will.

The devil will try to use people to dissuade and mislead you. James tells us that the tongue is the most powerful member of the body. People will say that you are making a mistake and that you won't succeed. They'll go as far as saying that "You'll never make it!" But I ask you, what did God say? As God told Jeremiah in Jeremiah 1:8, "Do not be afraid of their faces". They'll accuse the single women of trying to be like men and they'll accuse the married women of trying to take the leadership role in the family over her husband. Talk is no reason to wait. People will talk, yet you must walk. People talked and Noah kept on building the Ark. People talked and Nehemiah kept working on the wall. People talked and Jesus kept embracing the cross. People won't understand and you should not expect them to understand. It's not their calling. It's yours, you are the one expected to respond to it and speak positive about it. You won't understand their calling, not to the extent that they will. Likewise, they won't understand yours to the extent that you will. You cannot expect people to be able to relate to what God has told you.

They weren't there when He called you.

They weren't there when the Holy Spirit spoke to you. When He pricked your heart and set fire to every part of you that wanted to deny God. They weren't there when your spirit communed with the Holy Spirit.

They weren't there when the Power of God overwhelmed you as you cried "God, I love you. I'll go. I'll do whatever you want me to do".

No, they weren't there when the vision of the ministry flashed before your eyes and the Holy Spirit revealed God's will to you.

No, they weren't there when the Holy Spirit imparted God's instructions to you.

They weren't there when God encouraged you to go and the preached word confirmed your calling.

They were not there when you felt the call within the depths of your soul. So, let them talk. They were not there, but you were, and you should not wait.

❖

Faith, Not Fear

For God hath not given us the spirit of fear but of power, and of love, and of a sound mind.
2 TIMOTHY 1:7 KJV

Don't be afraid, God cannot fail. One of the biggest mistakes that we make as children of God is to measure our potential by our own physical and mental abilities and capabilities. As a result, the devil is allowed to use his greatest tool against us and that is fear. Fear of failure. I can't do this and I can't do that. No you cannot. That's why God is Creator, because you can only do through Him. Fear will try to latch on to you but you can't let it. Paul proclaimed in 1 John 4:46 *"He who is in you is greater than than he who is in the World."* and Philippians 4:13 "I can do all things through Christ who strengthens me." You are empowered by the Holy Spirit to succeed through Jesus Christ. That's why we must strive to be like Jesus. We are to be conformed to His image.

In Luke 19:1-5, Zacchaeus who was a rich tax collector and short in stature, sought to see Jesus. He didn't allow his shortness or any other disadvantage to deter him from seeing Jesus. He was driven by his innermost desire to see and know Jesus. We have to be willing to go where God sends us. Do anything to get to Jesus. We must be driven by our innermost desire to see and please God. Fear of failure has stopped many people, both male and female from venturing into ministries. It has stopped them from fulfilling God's purpose in their lives.

Oftentimes, we allow others to set the criterion for what is or is not success and who is or is not successful. Webster defines success as the "gaining of wealth, favor, or eminence." But God has already defined success for us. To you, a Christian, success is fulfilling the purpose that God has ordained for your life. And, in fulfilling this purpose, realizing that it involves allowing God to act on your behalf. It involves the realization that you are dependent on God and that He is the strength behind the power that causes one to achieve their divine purpose in Him. Success is to know God and the power of His salvation. Success is obeying God and as a result of this obedience, fulfilling His purpose for your life.

You must reject the devil's tool of fear and cling to God's tool of faith. In other words, faith not fear. God knows our potential and our availability to Him. He is omniscient. He knows how far we will go and how long it will take for us to get there. All you have to do is believe, then everything would be so much easier and you will fulfill God's purpose for your life.

I envision faith as being in a round shaped room that has no windows, no doors, no entrance, no exit, no cracks, no crevices in the walls, no floorboards, no fallout shelter. Just a perfectly rounded and closed in room, and I need to get out. The fact that I don't see a way out does not change the fact that I need to get out. I have nothing to go on but fear or faith. Fear says everything but I can. Faith says, I am your evidence that you will get out. It proclaims that God will make a way.

So much is not achieved because we don't have the faith to cause it to be done. And the thing about it is, God has given us more than we realize. But we are too scared to tap into the resources that He has given us to produce for Him. Don't you know that you have the power to speak things in and out of existence? Proverbs 18:21a is read, "Death and life is in the power of the tongue". What you speak out of your month can give life to a situation that should otherwise be dead or death to a situation that otherwise should have life. Whatever you choose to allow to come from your mouth is predicated on your faith in God.

Your calling from God is just that, a calling. You weren't waiting for it or expecting it, one day you just heard Him say go and you could not wait. The Bible tells us that to each is given a measure of faith by the Holy Spirit. It is your responsibility to utilize this faith. Maximize it. Take it to its fullest potential as ordained by God in your life. Not to recognize and do this is to abuse the gift that your creator has given you. Your measure is given to you based on God's foreknowledge of you. In Jeremiah 1:5, God tells Jeremiah that, "before I formed you in the womb I knew you; Before you were born I Sanctified you. I ordained you a prophet to the nations." The work is already done. You have been set up to perform God's purpose. In addition Romans 8:29 is read, "Whom He did foreknow, He predestined...." God, in His omniscience, before you were in your mother's womb knew you, your personality, the choices you would make including your decision to accept His gift of salvation. Oh yes, you were manifested in your mother's womb, but God created you long before your physical birth within the counsel of His own mind. During this time He predestined you. He predetermined and prearranged dates and times, people and even things such as buildings and land to create a season for your ministerial calling, for you to fulfill His purpose in your life. In other words, God has ordered your steps. This is why Isaiah proclaimed in 54:17a that no weapon formed against you can prosper and Paul in Romans 8:35-39 that nothing can separate you from the love of God which is in Christ Jesus our Lord. The enemy's tactic or weapon of fear, though formed, is of ill effect against a believing Christian. Your faith in God is an assurance that you will fulfill His purpose in your life. It is trusting without knowing. It is to believe in what God can do based on His ability not yours. So, all that you have to do, is choose faith not fear. Fear makes you wait. Faith makes you go because God said so.

❖

Left, But Not Gone

Though He slay me, yet will I trust Him
JOB 13:15

Sometimes we don't understand why God allows certain things to take place in our lives. But in the midst of our lack of understanding we hear Job encouraging us to trust God anyway. When the kids, cattle and friends are gone trust God. When those closest to you have nothing to offer but ridicule, misunderstanding, and misguided advice, trust God. When your spouse says, you can't, trust God. When it seems as though God has forsaken you and allowed chaos to break out not only around you but against you, trust God. Do not allow anybody or anything to separate you from the love of God. After everything that Job had been through, he still proclaimed," though HE slay me, yet will I trust Him." You must be convinced that whatever weapon the enemy has been allowed to form against you, if you trust God, it will not prosper.

Things aren't always as smooth between a husband and a wife as some would have you to believe when either one receives a call from God. The one receiving the call can become absorbed in the duty and excitement of the charge. Even to the point of selfishness, not realizing, that whether it's the husband or the wife who has received a call from God, it is a call that is intricately intertwined with the other spouse's calling, even if it doesn't appear to be so at that time. Therefore it is not about you, but what God is doing relative to both spouses as it relates to His divine plan for you individually and together. On the other hand, the one who has not received their calling as of yet or may have received their calling some time before, can have the tendency to feel left out or as if there is something out of order. We assume that God will operate in a way that we are use to or have been taught to, especially, in relation to a husband and wife. What we forget is that God is not a soap box derby God. You cannot ride Him anyway you want to. You must flow with Him and at His speed, not He with you nor at your speed. God is sovereign. He operates in the manner that pleases and glorifies Him.

Although my husband Darnell was with me in the beginning physically and seemingly spiritually, in reality, he was far from the ministry that God had placed on my heart to start. As a matter of fact, shortly after Word of God was birthed, Darnell left. Things didn't feel right to him and he had become very uncomfortable. Out of place so to speak. So he left. And there I was in pastoral ministry, yet I couldn't even keep my own husband in church. What an indictment, and if that wasn't enough, the church that Darnell had joined received him well and he became quite an active member there. He had become active in the youth ministry and he and the pastor (a man of course) appeared to have become close. He was an older and more seasoned Pastor. Darnell became very comfortable and content there and was allowed to minister the word on a number of occasions.

I found myself becoming annoyed, not only with Darnell, but also with the Pastor of the church. I felt that this Pastor should have encouraged Darnell to go home to Word of God Ministries. His interest should have been our healing. Instead, he tried to get him to join his church. Now that I think about it though, the pastor could only do what he knew. However, *GOD*, as always, is in control.

Yes, my husband Darnell left the ministry and there I was feeling betrayed, rejected, slain and left alone. But God set me straight quickly. He spoke to me and said, *"You do what I told you to do, and I'll take care of Darnell."* This promise let me know that yes Darnell had left, but he was not gone.

❖

Lord, Break Me

So I Said, Woe is me, for I am undone! Because I
am a man of unclean lips, And I dwell in the midst
of a people of unclean lips; for mine eyes have seen
the King, the LORD of hosts.
                                        ISAIAH 6:5

Brokenness is not a concept that most of us readily receive or grasp hold of. Yet, if we are sincere about our love
for God and our desire to do His will in our lives, then we'll
say, "Lord, break me" and we'll mean it. "Yes, Lord", we'll
profess, "Woe is me. I need to be mature in you."

It wasn't long before I knew that God wanted and intended
to break me. No matter how much I ranted and raved or
cried and kicked, I had to undergo the process of brokenness. I had to be emptied of the stuff in my life that did not
bring glory to God. He doesn't fill something that has holes
in it at both ends. But he repairs, patches, replaces, and then
proceeds to fill those areas of lack that must be filled in us.

Most of us are so self-preserving and full of ourselves that we keep our emotions and self-will or desires on a shelf where we don't want anyone-not even God-to touch them. We just let them sit until we are ready to open them up and expose them. We keep them preserved and protected, so we think. These emotions and areas of self-will are the untouchable areas of our lives, the comfort zones so to speak. They are areas where the Holy Spirit is not welcome, because we know that if He were to get hold of them, we would be exposed and changed. They would be emptied out because what God has in mind for us, and His idea of holiness doesn't mix with our nonsense, our stuff, nor our mess.

God's need and desire to break us can be seen in Luke 5:36 which tells us that you can't mix the new with the old. We can't put new wine into old skins. It just won't work. We are preserving pride, puffiness, unholy desires, bad attitudes, unforgiveness, and tradition and trying to mix them with the attributes and image of God, but it just won't work. And God won't allow it to either. We can't put those things on the shelf or allow them to lie dormant and please God at the same time. In Luke, the problem with the Pharisees was that they wanted business to go on as usual. They wanted Judaism to be the religion of the hour, the religion for everyone to measure their lives by. They didn't understand or even try to understand that Judaism couldn't accommodate Christianity. The two could not be mixed. Judaism lacked the character that accompanied Christianity. That character is Jesus Christ. Judaism didn't have His grace, mercy, or redemptive power.

Our old way of doing things lacks the mind and character of Jesus Christ. We must take that pride and selfishness off the shelf. They just won't mix with love and sacrifice. We must allow God to empty our preservatives and fill us with His character as listed in Galations 5:22:23 *"But the fruit of the Spirit is love, joy, peace, longsuffering, kindness, goodness, faithfullness, gentleness, selfcontrol"*

Even though it must be done, the process of being emptied will be painful and uncomfortable for sure. You will have to face the things about yourself that you have been comfortable with for so long. These are things that you either forgot about or have been enjoying so much that you just flat out deny its existence or refuse to give it up.

I submit to you though, that if you really love God, you will be like Isaiah, and cry "woe is me for I am of unclean lips." I acknowledge that God is awesome. At the same time, I acknowledge my own inadequacies. The presence of God causes me to look at myself and to examine the real me in me. And in examining myself I realize that I have problems and issues and I need to be changed. I need to be broken. I need to be emptied and filled by God.

❖

The Times I Could Have Quit

And Jesus said unto him, No man having put his hand to the plough, and looking back, is fit for the kingdom of God.

LUKE 9:62

As I mentioned before, my husband was with me in the beginning. He and I stood in front of a building in the rain and claimed it. It was one that we thought had the appearance of a church, so we figured that it would be easy to turn it into one. He was also present at the first service that was held at our home church. He was not only present, but he openly voiced his support. However, as I mentioned before, he changed shortly after we gave birth to Word of God Ministries.

While preaching I discerned a rebellious and contrary spirit suppressing him. He use to support me while I was preaching, but he had become totally silent and it had become obvious. He had gotten so bad that he wouldn't even look at me while I was preaching. And the inevitable finally happened. He left the church. And I kept on preaching as if nothing had happened. I could not let his absence stop me. I was sure of my call.

This period in the ministry was the opportune time for me to quit. I could have let doubt and frustration overwhelm me. But I couldn't. I was sure of my call. I did not wait and I could not quit.

No matter how things were, I could not look back as if God was not watching over His work. *I could not quit* or look back in doubt, frustration and uncertainty as if God could not produce fruit even out of my current condition. Looking back when God is saying go is not a posture that glorifies Him.

Darnell's absence had become noticeable. One of the members questioned me as to his absence or shall I say my inability as the pastor to keep him there. I can relate to what this person was thinking. How can I preach to her family if I can't keep mine in tact? How can I minister to her family members, if I can't minister to my own husband? How can I say God called me if I can't even keep my own husband in the church?

When we are faced with difficult situations and adversities, the first one that we should go to is God. Psalms 37:5 admonishes us to "Acknowledge the Lord in all thy ways and He shall direct your path." I think that this is especially true for pastors and others in leadership positions. It is our responsibility to God and our members to give our membership the right answer when they have a question. It's irresponsible to give them just any answer. We don't know how it will affect them and God will hold us accountable.

I had already sought God on this issue, so when the member mentioned above approached me, I settled it with her the same way God had settled it with me. I told her what

God had told me when I sought Him: "You focus on me, and I'll take care of Darnell." I ended with the understanding that I was going to do just that, focus on God.

I refused to dishonor God by trying to please others, by giving them a word or showing a reaction that God did not give me. Christians spend too much time trying to pacify others and too little time trying to please God.

What many who go into ministries don't expect-and even more so others who go with them-is for the pastor to have the same tendencies they had before entering the ministry. Yes, what I found surprising and even frustrating is that I didn't *automatically* become a mature pastor, but I had to grow into pastoral ministry. I was a pastor, but I still had sheep-like tendencies. I was a pastor but I was still prone to wander, to be irresponsible in some areas.

As a matter of fact, another time that I could have quit was when I realized that my biggest problem was my sheep like tendency to be closed off to people. I was not open to people, and that was not good, because I needed to fellow-ship with other people and other churches to build the ministry. My husband Darnell is much more of a people person than I am.

I could not understand why God called me, because I didn't have the pastoral personality, so to speak. But I was sure of my call so I could not quit. Although it was so hard to come out of my shell, the members were great and very receptive. They weren't the problem, I was and I could have quit. I didn't feel like putting forth the effort needed for me to change and fellowship. But my feelings were irrelevant. I could not quit. Instead, I was forced to grow up. The Holy Spirit caused me to examine myself and put away my toys. The child in me wanted to quit but I couldn't. God said no. I had to allow Him to break me in numerous areas of my life so that I could grow to the level of maturity that was necessary to effectively pastor a church and fulfill His purpose in my life.

I know what you're thinking. If I really loved God, I would have changed, unreluctantly. Not in the real flesh, my sister. I changed, but sometimes it was with reluctance. The flesh wants what it has been doing and it wants it now and it always will, at any cost. The flesh is not prone to reason. It is guided by emotions and desires relative to past experiences. This is why it must die daily so it cannot have rule over you.

Some areas of bondage lie dormant until you try to do something like starting a pastoral ministry. Personality traits begin coming out of the cracks and crevices of your heart. You wonder where did this come from and where did that come from? You know that it came from you and you will soon realize that you need to be refined in certain areas of your life so God can use you to the fullest.

Until I became a pastor, I hadn't realized I was such a procrastinator. I used to say that I did well under pressure and that's why I waited until the last minute to do things. When I was in school, I'd often wait until the night before to study for a test on the next day. As a matter of fact, I would often wait and study for the test that was being held in the class just before it. I usually did well too. I did well under pressure.

As a pastor, I found myself waiting too late to put programs together. People were not available or it was too rushed. Usually, the programs worked out okay, but I needed to change. This was quite clear even to me, so I know that my behavior was unacceptable to God. The truth of the matter is that I was a procrastinator and I could not quit.

When we enter into ministries for God, we have preconceived notions about how the ministry will grow. It's a given that pastors want their churches to grow, and we know that anything God plants will grow. But how and when, we don't decide and neither do we control. We can affect but not control.

Our preconceptions are usually based on tradition, lack of knowledge, and what we currently see or hear about. I read a book on church growth, how a church took in 200 members on their first Sunday, and now have over 10 thousand. My first Sunday was more like two. I found myself watching the numbers and before I knew it, I was judging my call by the numbers. When they didn't add up, *I could have quit.* My flesh wanted to quit. It was mentally laborious.

I knew people were judging my call by the numbers. If I was judging it that way, then surely they were too. It was natural. But that was the gist of the problem. It was a natural sign. I was looking at it in the natural and so were others. We are instructed to walk after the Spirit and not to mind the things of the flesh, yet my focus was on the physical and not the spiritual. I strove for spiritual maturity, growth, and development of the ministry, but when the time came to measure these factors, I did so in the physical. The physical cannot measure or comprehend the Spirit. What a mistake I made. What an insult to God. We must walk after the Spirit so we won't mind the things of the flesh.

❖

"Go"

The hand of the LORD came upon me and brought
me out in the Spirit of the LORD
EZEKIEL 37:1A

As the first anniversary celebration of Word of God Ministries approached, I knew I would be faced with the fact that people would soon learn that my husband had withdrawn his membership. Yes, he had joined another church, I could almost hear the echoes of people's voices ringing in my ear. "She couldn't even keep her own husband as a member. Surely this ministry is not an act of God or he would still be with her. God would not call the woman before her husband."

But this is why I said from the beginning, you must be sure, because without God the ministry would fail. When you have to embrace thoughts and principles, that don't sound doctrinal, you must be sure that God has truly called you.

I found myself seeking; not confirmation, but reassurance and even more so encouragement from God. Why, because He is God. Yes, I was sure that God had called me into this ministry, knowing that my husband would withdraw his support.

It is so important to keep a diary of your conversations with God, especially those that involve your calling from God and the instructions that relate to it. You will often need to reflect back on them for focus and reassurance.

You see, God had told me when He called me into the pastorate, "Go, even if you have to go alone." The two operative words were *go* and *alone*.

It was in the month of November 1997, during worship service at my home church, Randall Memorial Baptist Church. The service was of high praise as usual on Sunday mornings. I can remember standing, with my hands lifted in praise and praying to God, saying, "Lord, I'll do whatever you want me to do. I love you, Lord. I want to do your will in my life." My heart overflowed with love and adoration and the desire to do His will in my life.

As I spoke silently to God, with my eyes shut, I felt a hand on my shoulder. Our pastor, Dr. Earl Ross, had left the pulpit and gone to several people and prophesied to them. As he laid his hand on my shoulder, he said, "Peewee (my nickname), God said go, even if you have to go alone."

I nodded my head in the affirmative, letting him know that not only did I hear the message, but I received it also. Only God could have timed the message Pastor Ross gave me with the thoughts of my mind and the conversation that was taking place between God and me. All I could say was, "Yes, Lord, I'll go." Oh, how often do we find ourselves saying "yes, Lord," without knowing the details of the charge?

Even now I am reminded of a revival at Randall where a well-known evangelist was preaching and she posed a question in reference to being ready to be used by God. I can hear her repeatedly saying, "Are you ready?" And I can remember replying to God, "Yes, Lord, I'm ready." I can also remember God saying, "For everything?" "Yes, Lord," I said slowly, "for everything." God's tone, when He said the words "for everything," let me know that everything encompassed more than I could imagine then. Nevertheless, I yielded to the greater will. "Yes, Lord," I replied, "for everything."

About two weeks later, during worship service, God spoke to me again, as I lay prostrate on the floor before the pulpit. He repeatedly said, "Go, go now!" There was a burning within me so that I said, "Okay, Lord, I'll go, but where and to do what? How can I go when I don't know where to go?" Still not knowing where, I just said, "Okay, Lord, I'll go."

About a week after receiving my charge to go, during the evening worship service known as Hour of Power, Pastor Ross prophesied to two people, one of which was I. "Janice," Pastor Ross spoke, "God said that all the things (ministries) that you have done in the past, you will do again. You will bring them all together." He proceeded to say, "your friends will desert you but be encouraged." *Bless the Lord*, I thought to myself. I thought, what is them comprised of? Then I remembered "Them all" included plays, skits, and community outreach, which includes anything concerning the family structure. (youth outreach, alcohol and drug abuse outreach, family counseling, elderly assistance, 24 -Hour hotline, homeless shelter and women's ministry.)

I received another message during an intercessory prayer session at Randall. One of the ministers, now Pastor Phyllis Glascoe, Shachah Ministries in Beltsville, Maryland, prophesied to me: "God said get to packing. Pack your bags, you are about to travel." Well, the prophecy excited me because

I had already decided within myself that I was going to evangelize. Why evangelism? Because it was not restraining and it included traveling.

"Pack your bags; you are about to take a trip." Oh yes, I welcomed and received this message with open arms.

However, about a week or so later as I was ending my morning prayer, God spoke to me and said, "Janice, you are an angel." I remember thinking to myself, *Oh no, this is not the Lord. It's not scriptural. I am not an angel.* But God continued to speak: "You are my angel. Watch over and take care of my people."

At the same time a vision of an area appeared before me. I did not know the exact street, but I knew I would recognize it when I got to it. I didn't completely understand the message, although I knew it was God. My problem was that I was running late for work so I couldn't labor before God about it right then. As I hastened to shower, the Holy Spirit reminded me of the seven golden candlesticks that are spoken of in The Revelation. When God spoke to the churches in chapters 1-3, He addressed the pastors as angels. I was stunned. Oh my God, it was birthed in my spirit. I could hear the Holy Spirit revealing God's will to me. God wanted me to go. I was charged to birth a pastoral ministry.

The main reason I was stunned was because entering the pastoral ministry was the farthest thing from my mind. It did not include traveling, you see. Even then, I must admit, the traveling prophecy was now clear. I was going somewhere all right. I was going to leave my home church to birth another one.

My husband's support was not the only support I felt I lacked, but also my saved family members who had decided to remain at our home church. This not only hurt, but it was disappointing. Disappointing in the sense that we are a very close-knit family who always provide support for each other in our endeavors. Starting a new ministry required the need for support and hard workers; not to mention financial support. Because of our closeness, people just assumed that they would be going with me. I was hurt in the sense that I felt that I had always been there to support them, yet when my time came, they were not there for me. I felt that they didn't even seek God's will concerning their going, but just rejected the idea totally, and to me a rejection of the idea was a rejection of me. I was soon reminded, by the Holy Spirit, that it was not about me or my feeling of rejection, but I was destined to go without them. I had to learn how to depend solely on God.

"Go, even if you have to go alone." These words of prophecy that I received during a morning worship service soon rang strongly in my heart and spirit. The Holy Spirit ministered to me and I realized that God had ordained it for me. He had purposed these events to take place. It was not meant for my family to go with me, so even if they wanted to, He would not have allowed them to. I was destined to start the Word of God Ministries without my family's membership. It was in God's plan.

All too often we judge the actions of others, especially those close to us, by our physical emotions. By what we see and feel in the flesh. What we think ought to be happening. But if we were to rely on the Holy Spirit, especially at the most sensitive times to direct and instruct us, we wouldn't wear our feelings on our shoulders. We would be more in tune to God and we would understand what's going on in our lives and around us. We wouldn't make so many mistakes when things don't go our way.

The reason David is known for being a man after God's own heart and for walking in the ways of God was because he sought God so often. Even when he made mistakes, David sought God. He chased after God's love and delighted in praise and worship as well as His law. David always sought God, no matter what state he was in.

We need to understand that God ordains the events of a Christian's life. If we would just remember and take seriously the Rhema or personal word given to us by God, we would be more prepared when that word comes to pass.

I can remember when God first called me to preach. He also told me that I would be writing. Here I am over fifteen years later. Not only am I just beginning to write, but I am doing so as if God had never spoken to me about writing. When in actuality, I should have been building my writing skills. I should have been sharpening up on my language, speaking, etc. But no, I was chasing after other rainbows, such as sales, accounting, and even wanted to become a lawyer, only to see them not prosper because God had built His purpose inside of me and I have been, just as you are, ordained to fulfill it.

So, if you are about to go or are out there alone without the ones closest to you, don't be discouraged. You have all that you have been ordained to go with. God has chosen you for this ministry and you can't get all bent out of shape because of who does or does not go with you. Don't wait, the time is now! You just go with whomever God has blessed you to start with. Thank Him for who He has given you. Even if it's only yourself. "Give thanks for this is the will of God in Christ Jesus concerning you." Thank God and cherish those who are obedient, those He has blessed you with. There will be some who were supposed to go with you, but out of disobedience didn't, for one reason or another. Do not sweat it. Just sincerely pray for them and be about your business in God. I believe that we are in the last days before Jesus Christ comes back for the church. God is pouring His Spirit out upon all flesh. He desires male, female, children, and adults who will go because he told them to.

Someone asked me what, if anything, would I change about "going out"? I have come to understand that "go" involves a process of preparation. It includes a series of planning and pre-planting. It requires mental and physical preparation, as well as spiritual. God allows us to go to certain lengths in areas even though we are not yet knowledgeable in them. Why? Because stumbling and stammering is a part of our growth process. I know that it was necessary for me to reach a certain level of maturity so I would be able to take the wisdom and knowledge gained from my errors and apply them to my next assignments. I understand now that "go" involves a series of assignments that are vital to God's overall purpose for my life.

When God said "go,"He had predestined the bumps and bruises as well as the victories and healing that resulted from them. God starts with us, where we can meet Him and matures us to a level where He will meet us. Why should you wait? Just go.

❖

God Is Faithful

It is because of the Lord's mercies that we are not
consumed, because his compassions fail not. They
are new every morning; great is thy faithfulness.
LAMENTATIONS 3:22-23 KJV

I have learned that no matter how we feel or how un-
promising things may appear, how betrayed, slain, and left
alone we feel, God is faithful.

One Sunday morning about four months after Darnell
left Word of God Ministries, I looked up and there he was-
my husband-sitting in the *front* seat. I tell you, if you will let
go and let God, things will work out. God will take care of
everything. He will do just as He says He will. God had told
me, "You do what I told you to do and I'll take care of Darnell."
And He did just that.

At home I barely mentioned Word of God Ministries and
Darnell barely mentioned the church he was attending. No,
we didn't sleep in separate bedrooms. We just left the church
at church when we were in each other's company. I kept study-

ing, pastoring, and praising God just as He told me to do. I stayed focused on Him and left the impossible and improbable to Him. You know what He did? Just what He said He would do. He took care of Darnell.

God is faithful. We are the ones who are prone to wander. We do so especially when things don't go our way or look as if they are unmanageable. Like sheep, we just go astray. And God? He remains faithful.

❖

Because I Could Trust You to Move

"Trust in the LORD with all your heart, And lean
not on your own understanding."
PROVERBS 3:5

Some two years later after giving birth to Word of God
Ministries, I sat in my home church, Randall Ministries, during an afternoon service. As Pastor Ross acknowledged the
visiting clergy and their represented churches, I felt a tug-
ging at my Spirit. I felt out of place and uncomfortable with
being in a leadership position over my husband. At this point
Darnell had not only become active in the ministry, but he
was stepping into the leadership position in the church. He
didn't realize it, but I did. I had observed how God was
positioning him to step into the pastoral ministry. I didn't
say anything to Him or anyone else, except my best friend
Minister Charmaine Gibson. I had confided in her because
she understood the moves of God and she was unbiased. God
not only brought Darnell back to Word of God but He sanctified him. Darnell had grown so much spiritually. My being
publicly acknowledged above Darnell had happened many

times before and it didn't bother me or for the most part
Darnell either. He came back accepting my pastoral leadership of Word of God Ministries. Yet that day I felt a tug at my
Spirit that not even I can describe. The discomfort I felt that
day not only continued but became more intense. So, I went
to God. I knew in my spirit that God was about to make a
switch between Darnell and myself with the pastoral leadership.

Now, anyone starting a church knows that it's a lot of
work, prayer, commitment, dedication, and sacrifice. And
usually when a person puts these components into something they have an attachment to it and are not readily anxious
to give it up. To receive any inkling to give up control of
something that you built from the ground up can be a bit
distressing. So I went to the Lord, not in rebellion, but quite
frankly, I couldn't understand why He didn't just use Darnell
in the first place.

"Lord," I asked respectfully, "why did You have me go
through all of this and then give the pastoral to Darnell?"
God responded in His still, but authoritative voice, *"Because
I could trust you to move."* All I needed was an answer. I got it
and I moved. Just as God said go and I did not wait, when
He said move, I did not wait either. I moved.

Today, after six years, Word of God Ministries, under the
pastoral ministry of Darnell and Janice Fountaine, is grow-
ing where it is planted. We also gave birth to the Restore
Community Development Center through which we had the
opportunity to host a summer youth program for three years.
During that time we helped the youth produce *From One Teen
to Another* magazine and "Tell It Like It Is in the Name of the
Lord" teen talk show and group sessions.

In addition, God has given me an awesome vision for broken women. Women Empowered to Support Other Women Worldwide-W.E.S.O.W.-is a worldwide network of women's ministries designed to help the unsaved come into a saving relationship with God and to help the saved come into a more intimate relationship with Him. Our charge is to help women birth the ministries God has ordained for their lives, through preaching, teaching, seminars and other support ministries, both will be encouraged to sow into the harvest of other broken women locally and internationally.

God has a purpose and a plan for all of our lives. This plan is incubated in His universal plan for His kingdom. It is our responsibility to hear and obey Him-no matter what we think the cost will be or our ability to understand or comprehend His intentions and will. I realize now, more so than ever, that I could not wait. God has a blueprint and a schedule for our lives and ministries. My blueprint includes Pastors Darnell Fountaine and Janice Fountaine, Word of God Ministries, and the community in which we are housed-as well as other ministries and assignments that are within the scope of my calling and purpose in God.

I thank and glorify God continuously for being sovereign and for ordaining me to be a part of His plan. Why Should I Wait?

Prayer of Acceptance

Dear Heavenly Father, I acknowledge you as creator and Lord of and over my life. You are an awesome God and I love you more than anyone or anything. I accept your call on my life to _____.
Thank you for considering me for your work and allowing me the opportunity to glorify you.

Father, I submit myself to you in all areas of my life. Mold me, I pray, into the very essence of you. Cause me, Father, to be exactly what you want me to be so that I will always glorify you as I fulfill your purpose in my life. I pray this prayer, father, knowing that the Holy Spirit will set fire to the areas of my life that need to be purified. He will move the obstacles that need to be moved and set in order the areas that need to be in submission.

Walk me through the challenges that I must endure and conquer, Father. Cause me now, Holy Spirit, to embrace my empowerment from you to fulfill my ordained purpose in Christ Jesus.

Thank you Father, in Jesus' name I pray, amen.

To order additional copies of

WHY SHOULD I WAIT?

When God Said Go!

have your credit card ready and call
1 800-917-BOOK (2665)

or e-mail
orders@selahbooks.com

or order online at
www.selahbooks.com

Janice Fountaine
W.E.S.O.W.
P.O. Box 5162
Hyattsville, MD 20782
(301) 277-0640

www.ingramcontent.com/pod-product-compliance
Lightning Source LLC
Chambersburg PA
CBHW031611040426
42452CB00006B/479